Wolfgang Gula

Plants for
Your Aquarium

With photos by renowned
aquarium photographers
Illustrations:
Johann Brandstetter

2 CONTENTS

TYPICAL
AQUARIUM PLANTS

- Create an actual underwater landscape in the aquarium.

- Provide for constantly changing scenery in the aquarium as they grow.

- Supply oxygen, without which there would be no life in the water.

- Help to maintain the biological equilibrium in the aquarium.

- Remove toxins from the water and create a healthy aquatic environment.

- Mark territorial boundaries for many species of fish.

- Provide hiding places for fry.

Hobbyists have long known that a beautiful, diverse landscape is extremely important for an aquarium. But a healthy plant community featuring a wide variety of species is not merely a delight to the eye; it also performs many complex biological functions. If the plants are thriving in an aquarium, you can assume that the underwater conditions are suitable for most other forms of life as well. Growing plants not only produce abundant amounts of oxygen, which is essential for life, they also remove many contaminants from the water. Some of these substances, such as nitrate, are used for the synthesis of plant tissue; others, like heavy metals or many pesticides, are stored in plant organs and thus rendered permanently harmless to all but plant-eating species.

Lush vegetation transforms an aquarium into a naturalistic habitat for most species of ornamental fish. Aquatic plants give the tank structure, making it easier for the fish to orient themselves and establish territorial boundaries. They create shady shelters, offer suitable spawning sites, and provide places for baby fish to hide from predatory tankmates. And even aquarists who are primarily interested in fish know how important plants are for a biotope aquarium.

SELECTING AQUARIUM PLANTS

Aquatic plants are far more than just decorative accessories for tropical fish—they perform many vital functions in the freshwater aquarium. Choosing the right species makes it easier to achieve a state of biological equilibrium in which all living things are happy.

Why an Aquarium Needs Plants

The simplest answer would be: "Because they look so pretty." But that's also true of ornamental fish or a decorative root. The importance of underwater flora goes far beyond that.

No life without oxygen: One of the most important tasks of aquarium plants is the liberation of oxygen through a process known as photosynthesis. Just as on land, plants in the water can use light as a source of energy and, with the help of chlorophyll, the green pigment found in their leaves, transform carbon dioxide (CO_2) and water into carbohydrates and oxygen. Carbohydrates are used to synthesize plant tissue and to store energy. Oxygen is released into the water, where it is available to animals and microorganisms for respiration. Incidentally, plants respire around the clock, so they must make enough oxygen during the day to supply all the aquarium's inhabitants through the night. [Note: This is not the only source of dissolved oxygen in water, as most of the O_2 enter at the surface by a process of gas exchange.]

Fanwort (Cabomba aquatica) is a stem plant that has finely divided leaves. Flowers are rarely produced under aquarium conditions.

Plants for a healthy environment: In an aquarium, large quantities of nitrogen compounds accumulate. They come from leftover food as well as from fish excrement. Special microorganisms break down these compounds into a form that can be taken up by the plants as "fertilizer." Because plants absorb nitrógen compounds as well as many other harmful substances in the water like pesticides, fish medications, and heavy metals, thus rendering them harmless, they assume the job of waste removal in the aquarium, so to speak. [Note: This does not eliminate the need for regular partial water changes.] In addition, they create a healthy environment: Thriving aquarium plants are the best method for suppressing the troublesome growth of algae.

Habitat structures: Plants provide aquarium fish with all sorts of hiding places. They make it easier for many fish species to define their territorial boundaries, and they provide suitable sites for spawning.

Only in rare cases does it make sense to have an aquarium without plants (for example, quarantine tanks). The beneficial effects for all organisms and the many design possibilities justify taking time to plan and maintain a planted aquarium.

Origin and Ecology of Aquarium Plants

The term "aquarium plants" refers to all those species which can be kept in the aquarium permanently. In addition to the actual aquatic plants, these include a wide range of marsh and bog plants that will survive when fully submerged.

True aquatic plants can grow underwater throughout the year—this type of growth is called "submersed." The stems and leaves of these species have a system of air-filled vessels that gives the entire plant the necessary buoyancy. The leaves are usually delicate and thin and often finely divided. In this way, aquatic plants reduce their resistance to the current and increase the surface area of their leaves, through which they absorb most of the substances required for their growth. A typical example of this type is Dwarf Ambulia (*Limnophila sessiliflora*) (→ page 23). In many aquatic plants, the roots are no longer needed for uptake of nutrients—they serve merely to anchor the plant or else are greatly reduced.

Swamp and bog plants are amphibious: only during the wet season do they live in a completely submersed state; when the water level drops, they stand partially or completely above water. This type of growth is called "emersed." The transformation from one state to the other leads to more or less significant changes in appearance. In most species, the submersed parts of the plant are decidedly more delicate in structure, even though in comparison with true aquatic plants they are coarser and less finely divided. The roots of all amphibious plants play an important role in nutrient uptake, which is why the aquarium substrate must be adequately fertilized (→ page 51).

Special habitats:

✔ Floating plants, like Water Lettuce (*Pistia stratiotes*) (→ page 25), can drift on the surface of the water because they store air in their tissues. They extract required nutrients from the water with the help of their fine roots.

✔ The spray zone of waterfalls is an extreme habitat which has been colonized by a few species like the Java Fern (*Microsorium pteropus*) (→ page 24) and the African Fern (*Bolbitis heudelottii*).

Selecting and Buying Plants

The greater the selection, the harder it is to choose. This is certainly true of selecting plants for the home aquarium. Pet stores usually offer a wide assortment of plants, which delights aquarium lovers, but also presents some major problems.

Selection Criteria

Choosing the right plants is no easy task considering the bewildering variety of species. Be sure to take advantage of the expert advice you'll get at the pet store and consider the following important criteria in order to maintain a lushly planted, biologically stable aquarium.

✔ If you want to keep aquarium maintenance to a minimum, choose mostly rosette plants (→ page 14).

✔ When selecting plants, always keep the size of your aquarium in mind. Rampantly growing plants are not a good idea for small tanks—they would quickly fill up the available space. However, don't choose only large species for large aquariums. Plants of different heights will create a feeling of depth and provide for a more natural appearance.

✔ Most aquarium plants look best in groups. Only true specimen plants like the Red Tiger Lotus (*Nymphaea lotus*) (→ page 18) should be planted by themselves.

✔ Approximately half of the plants you select should be fast-growing species. These contribute substantially more to healthy conditions in the aquarium.

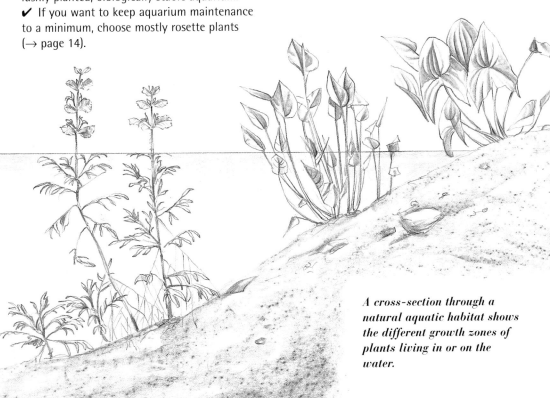

A cross-section through a natural aquatic habitat shows the different growth zones of plants living in or on the water.

Checklist
What to Look for When Buying

When buying aquarium plants, make sure that, by and large, the following are true:

1 The aquarium plants offered for sale are in well-tended, well-lit display tanks.

2 Each individual plant is tagged with an easy-to-read label (common and scientific names, type).

3 The store has a large assortment of plants for sale, and there are several plants of each species to choose from.

4 The plants—stems and leaves—are free from feeding damage or other injuries.

5 The leaves are a uniform deep green (or the normal color for the species).

6 The leaves and stems are not overgrown with algae.

7 No brown leaves or other discolorations are visible on the plants.

✔ In order to ensure steady, luxuriant growth, the plants you select should have more or less similar requirements for light, temperature, and water quality.

✔ If you want to keep certain species of fish, this can drastically limit your choice of plants. For instance, discus need relatively high water temperatures and many cichlids require hard water—conditions that not all aquarium plants can tolerate. If you want to keep schooling fish which need plenty of swimming room, tall or spreading plants are suitable only for the background.

✔ If you are considering a biotope aquarium, i.e., a reproduction of a specific natural habitat, then you should choose only plants and fish from the same geographic region that go together well.

Transporting Aquarium Plants

When you have finally selected and purchased your plants, you still have to get them home intact. At the pet store, the plants will usually be packed wet in a plastic bag for you. That will suffice for a short trip home, but always bear in mind that aquarium plants are very delicate:

✔ Never leave the plant bag in the sun, otherwise the plants can easily overheat.

✔ In winter, the plant bag must be wrapped in several sheets of newspaper or some other insulating material.

Important: Once home, put the plants in warm water (20 to maximum 25°C [68 to 77°F]) as soon as possible.

Plants in Portrait

The following Portraits will acquaint you with a sampling of adaptable aquarium plants which are available in most pet stores. Generally speaking, aquarists distinguish between rosette plants and stem plants because of differences in the care they require. Plants with special growth forms are presented in the third section of the Portraits. In addition, you will find important information on the selection and care of each species (references to photos follow the Latin name):

✔ A brief description of the species and its use in the aquarium.
✔ Its geographic origin.

A diverse community of aquarium plants competing for the available space.

✔ Temperature and light requirements.
✔ Special notes on care.
✔ Alternative, similar-to-care-for species.
   Any attempt to organize the plants according to pH and water hardness was deliberately avoided. With optimal monitoring and adjustment of the water quality, as explained in the second chapter (→ page 29), all species described in this book will accept similar pH and water hardness values. See the information in the chapter on water quality (→ page 36).

14 Selecting Aquarium Plants

Rosette Plants

In botany, species whose leaves all originate from a single base are called rosette plants. Viewed from above, these plants have the appearance of a rosette—hence the name. You can find additional information on this group in the chapter on plant care (→ page 49).

Dwarf Anubias

Anubias barteri var. *nana* (→ photo, page 16)
Slow-growing, low, decidedly robust species for the foreground or for tying onto bogwood and rocks (→ page 46).
Origin: Tropical Africa.
Temperature: 22 to 26°C (72 to 79°F).
Light requirement: Low.
Special note: Because they are so indestructible, anubias are classic plants for the cichlid tank.

Similar to care for: *Anubias afzelii, A. gracilis, A. barteri* var. *barteri, A. heterophylla, A. lanceolata, A. congensis.*

Water Sprite, Indian Fern

Ceratopteris thalictroides (→ photo, page 37)
Very fast-growing fern with finely cut, light green leaves for the background.
Origin: Indonesia, Southeast Asia.
Temperature: 22 to 28°C (72 to 82°F).
Light requirement: Moderate.
Special note: Especially suitable for concealing filters and heaters in the aquarium.
Similar to care for: *Hygrophila difformis.*

Ruffled Ribbon Cryptocoryne

Cryptocoryne crispatula var. *balansae* (→ photo, page 17)
Easy-care, relatively slow-growing species for the middleground; its puckered leaves, up to 30 cm (12 inches) long, make it an eye-catcher.
Origin: India, Southeast Asia.
Temperature: 20 to 26°C (68 to 79°F).
Light requirement: Low to moderate.
Special note: Many varieties with leaves of various widths are available.
Similar to care for: *Cryptocoryne spiralis, C. undulata, C. aponogetifolia, C. retrospiralis, C. tonkiniensis.*

Wendt's Cryptocoryne

Cryptocoryne wendtii (→ photo, page 17)
Fast-growing foreground plant which quickly forms dense stands; ideal for new setups.

Several varieties of **Nymphaea lotus** *are available in pet stores.*

Origin: Sri Lanka, Southeast Asia.
Temperature: 22 to 26°C (72 to 79°F).
Light requirement: Rather low.
Special note: Green- and brown-leaved forms.
Similar to care for: *Cryptocoryne walkeri,*
C. beckettii, C. moehlmanii.

Willis' Cryptocoryne
Cryptocoryne × willisii (→ photo, page 17)
Slow-growing foreground plant.
Origin: Sri Lanka, India.
Temperature: 22 to 28°C (72 to 82°F).
Light requirement: Moderate to high.
Special note: Looks more delicate than it is.
Similar to care for: *Cryptocoryne lucens,*
C. nevillii, C. parva.

Broad-leaf Amazon Swordplant
Echinodorus bleheri (→ photo, page 16)
Very large, fast-growing specimen plant for the
middleground.
Origin: South America.
Temperature: 22 to 28°C (72 to 82°F).
Light requirement: Moderate.
Special note: Requires plenty of nutrients—so
fertilize regularly (→ page 51).
Similar to care for: *Echinodorus amazonicus,*
E. parviflorus, E. martii.

Radicans Swordplant
Echinodorus cordifolius (→ photo, page 16)
Very large, fast-growing plant with broad
leaves.
Origin: North, South, and Central America.
Temperature: 20 to 28°C (68 to 82°F).
Light requirement: Moderate to high.
Special note: In open aquariums, its large
leaves extend out of the water.
Similar to care for: *Echinodorus schlüteri,*
E. osiris (→ photo, page 61), *E. horizontalis*
(→ photo, page 44), *E. barthii.*

TIP

Not Suitable for the Aquarium

Sometimes dealers sell plants for the
aquarium which are entirely unsuitable
for this habitat. These are usually just
houseplants that will soon die underwater.
Examples of such species are
Chinese Evergreen (*Aglaonema* species)
Fancy-leaved Caladium (*Caladium bicolor*
hybrids)
Spider Plant (*Chlorophytum comosum*)
Umbrella Plant (*Cyperus alternifolius*)
Ti Plant (*Cordyline terminalis*)
Dumb Cane (*Dieffenbachia* species)
Belgian Evergreen (*Dracaena sanderiana*)
Nerve Plant (*Fittonia verschaffeltii*)
Polka-dot Plant (*Hypoestes phyllostachya*)
Wild Asian Grass (*Peliosanthes* species)
Philodendron (*Philodendron* species)
Artillery Plant (*Pilea vanderi*)
Golden Pothos (*Scindapsus aureus*)
Spikemoss (*Selaginella* species).

Broad-leaf Chain Swordplant, Dwarf Amazon Swordplant
Echinodorus quadricostatus (→ photo, page 17)
Bright green, moderately fast-growing fore-
ground plant with plentiful runners.
Origin: Central and South America.
Temperature: 22 to 28°C (72 to 82°F).
Light requirement: High.
Special note: Susceptible to iron deficiency
disease (→ page 53).
Similar to care for: *Echinodorus tenellus,*
E. bolivianus, Sagittaria platyphylla, Eleocharis
parvula.

IN PORTRAIT:
ROSETTE PLANTS

In rosette plants, the leaves grow from a single crown. The leaves themselves sit on leaf stems, or petioles, of varying lengths, which may be absent in some species.

The Radicans Swordplant (Echinodorus cordifolius) needs plenty of space in the aquarium.

Straight Vallisneria (Vallisneria spiralis) forms a dense wall of green in the aquarium.

Photo below: Dwarf Anubias (Anubias barteri var. nana).

Photo right: Broad-leaf Amazon Sword-plant (Echinodorus bleheri).

Photo left: The more light Broad-leaf Chain Swordplant (**Echinodorus quadricostatus**) *gets, the faster and more luxuriantly it grows.*

Photo above: Wendt's Cryptocoryne (**Cryptocoryne wendtii**) *thrives in almost any aquarium.*

Photo above: Dwarf Sagittaria (**Sagittaria subulata**).

Photo left: Willis' Cryptocoryne (**Cryptocoryne × willisii**).

Photo above: Ruffled Ribbon Cryptocoryne (**Cryptocoryne crispatula**).

Red Tiger Lotus

Nymphaea lotus rubra (→ photo, page 2/3)
Fast-growing, very attractive specimen plant for larger aquariums.
<u>Origin:</u> Central Africa, Madagascar.
<u>Temperature:</u> 22 to 28°C (72 to 82°F).
<u>Light requirement:</u> High.
<u>Special note:</u> In bright light, develops floating leaves on long stems which extend up to the water surface; they shade the aquarium and must be removed regularly (→ HOW-TO: Plant Care, pages 58/59)..
<u>Similar to care for:</u> *Nymphaea lotus* 'Green', *Nymphaea stellata*.

Dwarf Sagittaria, Narrow-leaf Sagittaria

Sagittaria subulata (→ photo, page 17)
Fast-growing foreground plant which remains low; reproduces by means of runners and forms a regular underwater lawn.
<u>Origin:</u> Eastern USA, South America.
<u>Temperature:</u> 18 to 28°C (64 to 82°F).
<u>Light requirement:</u> Moderate.
<u>Special note:</u> Thin the stand from time to time so that the plants don't grow too tall.
<u>Similar to care for:</u> *Lilaeopsis novae-zelandiae, Glossostigma elatinoides, Echinodorus tenellus.*

Straight Vallisneria

Vallisneria spiralis (→ photo, page 16)
The ideal background plant because of its narrow leaves, which grow straight up; reproduces by runners that creep across the bottom and quickly form dense stands.
<u>Origin:</u> Asia, Africa, Australia.
<u>Temperature:</u> 20 to 28°C (68 to 82°F).
<u>Light requirement:</u> Low to moderately high.
<u>Special note:</u> The name *"spiralis"* refers to the spiraling female flower stem which extends or retracts depending on the water level.
<u>Similar to care for:</u> *Vallisneria* 'contorcionist', *V. gigantea, V. asiatica.*

Plant path composed of 1 Cardinal Flower, 2 Dwarf Rotala, 3 Amazon Swordplant.

Stem Plants

In botany, species whose leaves grow on a creeping or upright stem are called stem plants. In contrast to rosette plants, they have no fixed center of growth, but rather keep getting longer and, in most species, branch as well. Plants having this pattern of growth require more care from the aquarist, since they must be rejuvenated regularly and their height has to be kept in check (→ chapter on plant care, page 49).

Red Hygrophila

Alternanthera reineckii 'Rosaefolia' (→ photo, page 48)

Attractive, fast-growing red to purple middleground plant.

Origin: Southeast Asia.

Temperature: 22 to 28°C (72 to 82°F).

Light requirement: Moderate to high (high levels of light encourage redness).

Special note: Disproves the claim that red-leaved plants are difficult to grow.

Similar to care for: *Alternanthera cardinalis, A. sessilis, Rotala macranta, Ammania gracilis* (→ photo, page 52).

Giant Bacopa, Water Hyssop

Bacopa caroliniana (→ photo, page 20)

Relatively fast-growing middleground plant with attractive, olive-green, fleshy leaves.

Origin: Southeastern USA, Central America.

Temperature: 20 to 26°C (68 to 79°F).

Light requirement: Moderate to high.

Special note: In bright light the leaves turn somewhat brownish. The plant is especially attractive when pruned back irregularly to different heights.

Similar to care for: *Bacopa monnieri, Lysimachia nummularia.*

Green Cabomba, Carolina Fanwort

Cabomba caroliniana (→ photo, page 25)

By far the most frequently sold fast-growing stem plant; well supplied with light and nutrients, it forms large decorative thickets in the background. It offers baby fish good protection from predatory tankmates.

Origin: Eastern USA, South America.

Temperature: 20 to 25°C (68 to 77°F).

Light requirement: Moderate to high.

*Special note: This is a fairly demanding plant to keep in your aquarium. If light is inadequate, it will become leggy and unattractive. It also dislikes heat.

Similar to care for: *Cabomba aquatica* (→ photo, page 8), *C. piauhyensis, Myriophyllum aquaticum, M. scabratum, Ceratophyllum submersum.*

Anacharis, Giant Elodea

Egeria (Elodea) densa (→ photo, page 21)

This best-known aquatic plant grows very quickly; used either in the background or as a floating plant; produces very few roots.

Origin: Cosmopolitan.

Temperature: 10 to 24°C (50 to 75°F).

Light requirement: Moderate to high.

Special note: Because it is very tolerant of water quality, Anacharis is ideal for new setups; in the long run, however, the plant has problems with the high temperatures in tropical aquariums.

Similar to care for: *Lagarosiphon major, Elodea crispa.*

IN PORTRAIT:
STEM PLANTS

Stem plants, in contrast to rosette plants, do not have a central growing point, or crown. As the stem grows, the plants increase in height and produce more leaves on new stems.

*Photo above: Water Wisteria (**Hygrophila difformis**) needs plenty of room to develop.*

*Photo above: Shade Mudflower (**Micranthemum umbrosum**).*

*Photo right: Giant Hygrophila (**Hygrophila corymbosa**).*

*Photo left: Giant Bacopa (**Bacopa caroliniana**) is only effective in groups.*

Photo left: Ludwigia palustris × L. repens *displays an intense red color on the undersides of the leaves.*

Photo above: Dwarf Ambulia (Limnophila sessiliflora) should be included in every newly planted tank.

Photo above: Hygrophila polysperma 'Rosanervig' *is a variety of Dwarf Hygrophila.*

Photo above: Cardinal Flower forms round green leaves underwater.

Photo left: Anacharis (Egeria densa) is a good oxygenator, but best kept in a cool water aquarium.

Brazilian Pennywort
Hydrocotyle leucocephala (→ photo, pages 6/7)
Fast-growing background plant for larger
aquariums; very attractive because of its un-
usual leaf form and the roots growing from the
leaf axils.
Origin: South America.
Temperature: 18 to 28°C (64 to 82°F).
Light requirement: Low to high.
Special note: Also grows as a floating plant at
the water surface and then provides a great
deal of shade.
Similar to care for: *Hydrocotyle verticillata*,
Cardamine lyrata (→ photo, page 33).

Giant Hygrophila
Hygrophila corymbosa (→ photo, page 20)
Fast-growing plant for grouping in the middle-
ground of large aquariums.
Origin: Southeast Asia.
Temperature: 22 to 28°C (72 to 82°F).
Light requirement: Moderate to high.
Special note: Sometimes loses a few leaves
after being planted, but usually leafs out again
quickly.
Similar to care for: *Hygrophila siamensis, H.
salicifolia.*

Water Wisteria
Hygrophila difformis (→ photo, page 20)
Fast-growing plant for the aquarium middle-
ground with striking, highly pinnate leaves; be
sure to give it plenty of space.
Origin: India, Thailand, Malaysia.
Temperature: 22 to 28°C (72 to 82°F).
Light requirement: Moderate.
Special note: Also sold under the names
Vistaria and *Synema.*
Similar to care for: *Hygrophila difformis*
'Green-White', *Ceratopteris thalictroides.*

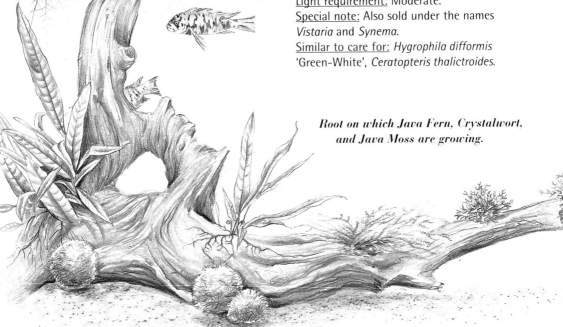

*Root on which Java Fern, Crystalwort,
and Java Moss are growing.*

Dwarf Hygrophila

Hygrophila polysperma (→ photo, page 21)
Robust, fast-growing plant for the background and middleground.
Origin: India.
Temperature: 22 to 28°C (72 to 82°F).
Light requirement: Moderate.
Special note: Ideal stem plant for beginners; grows quickly in almost any water conditions and is extremely easy to propagate.
Similar to care for: *Hygrophila polysperma* 'Rosanervig', *Heteranthera zosterifolia*, *Alternanthera sessilis*.

Dwarf Ambulia

Limnophila sessiliflora (→ photo, page 21)
Especially fast growing and therefore an excellent plant for the middleground and background of new setups (→ page 41).
Origin: Asia.
Temperature: 20 to 26°C (68 to 79°F).
Light requirement: High.
Special note: Its growth keeps that of algae in check.
Similar to care for: *Limnophila aquatica*, *Hottonia inflata*.

Cardinal Flower

Lobelia cardinalis (→ photo, page 21)
Undemanding aquarium plant which doesn't grow too quickly; best suited for so-called plant paths (→ HOW-TO: Plant Care, pages 58/59).
Origin: North America.
Temperature: 22 to 26°C (72 to 79°F).
Light requirement: Moderate.
Special note: Flowers on plants grown emersed quickly lose the cardinal red coloring.
Similar to care for: *Ludwigia arcuata*, *Eustralis stellata* (→ photo, page 56).

Broad-leaf Ludwigia

Ludwigia palustris × L. repens
(→ photo, page 20)
Attractive, fast-growing plant with reddish brown leaves; should be placed in small groups in the background or middleground.
Origin: USA, Mexico.
Temperature: 23 to 28°C (73 to 82°F).
Light requirement: Moderate to high.
Special note: The underside of the leaf is a more intense red than the upper side. The red coloring is helped along by bright light.
Similar to care for: *Ludwigia glandulosa*, *L. perennis*.

Shade Mudflower

Micranthemum umbrosum (→ photo, page 20)
Extremely small-leaved foreground plant that resembles the houseplant "Baby's Tears."
Origin: USA.
Temperature: 20 to 24°C (68 to 75°F).
Light requirement: High.
Special note: With good carbon dioxide fertilization, the plant grows quite quickly and forms masses of oxygen bubbles on its leaves.
Similar to care for: *Glossostigma elatinoides*, *Micranthemum micranthemoides*.

Dwarf Rotala

Rotala rotundifolia (→ photo, page 37)
Fast-growing, attractive plant for grouping in the middleground; as with most red-leafed aquatic plants, the brighter the light, the redder the leaves.
Origin: Southeast Asia.
Temperature: 22 to 28°C (72 to 82°F).
Light requirement: Moderate to bright.
Special note: Grows in soft and hard water.
Similar to care for: *Rotala walichii*, *Mayaca fluviatilis*.

The roots of Water Lettuce form an exquisite network in the water.

Plants with Special Growth Forms

Many aquarium plants cannot be classified as either stem plants or rosette plants. Included in this group are a few fern species adapted to very special habitats, plants which float on the water surface, and some higher algae.

Lake Ball, Marimo Ball

Cladophora aegagropila (→ photo, page 53)
Colonies of an algal species which look very decorative when placed in the foreground; easy to care for and extremely slow growing.
Origin: Eastern Europe, East Asia.

Temperature: 0 to 24°C (32 to 75°F).
Light requirement: Moderate.
Special notes: Lake Balls are veritable biological filters: They provide a home for vast numbers of microorganisms which in turn purify the water. These plants are almost never commonly sold in the U.S.

Java Fern

Microsorium pteropus
Robust, rather slow-growing aquarium plant specialized for life in the spray zone of waterfalls. The weakly developed roots can no longer absorb nutrients, but serve only to anchor the

plant; therefore it can easily be tied onto roots or stones (→ page 46).
Origin: Java, Indonesia.
Temperature: 20 to 28°C (68 to 82°F).
Light requirement: Low to moderate.
Special note: One of the few fern species among the aquarium plants, these are very easily grown under a variety of conditions.
Similar to care for: *Bolbitis heudelottii, Microsorium pteropus* 'Windelov'.

Water Lettuce

Pistia stratiotes (→ photo, pages 24, 49)
A true floating plant in which all parts except for the roots grow above the water surface. Especially attractive are the filigreed roots which develop in the water. These are an ideal hiding place for fry and are used as a spawning site by various species of aquarium fish.
Origin: Throughout the tropics.
Temperature: 22 to 30°C (72 to 86°F).
Light requirement: Moderate.
Special note: This heavy feeder absorbs large amounts of nitrogen from the water through its roots and thus reduces the danger of excessive algal growth. The more closely spaced the plants, the faster Water Lettuce reproduces. This plant tends to fare very poorly in aquariums.
Similar to care for: *Salvinia auriculata, Limnobium laevigatum.*

Crystalwort

Riccia fluitans (→ photo, page 53)
One of the most mysterious of the aquarium plants: The tiny, bifurcating ribbons of plant tissue form balls that usually float on the surface. Occasionally they produce cushions underwater, as well, but the mechanism of this independent change of habitat is still not completely understood. In the aquarium, the plants can be induced to form underwater cushions by fastening them to roots with netting or nylon thread. Given enough light, Crystalwort spreads quickly.
Origin: Cosmopolitan.
Temperature: 20 to 27°C (68 to 81°F).
Light requirement: High.
Special note: The floating balls serve as spawning sites for labyrinth fish.
Similar to care for: *Vesicularia dubyana.*

A large thicket of Green Cabomba (**Cabomba caroliniana**).

HOW-TO: SAMPLE PLANT LAYOUTS

Community Aquarium (120 × 50 × 50 cm) (48 × 20 × 20 inches)

Plants of contrasting colors and shapes can be assembled to form a natural-looking underwater landscape that is broken up by open areas and decorative roots or rocks. Despite lush vegetation, fish have plenty of room to swim in all areas.

Sample plant layout (50 plants)

✔ For the background:
5 plants *Vallisneria spiralis*
5 bunches *Cabomba caroliniana*
5 bunches *Hygrophila polysperma*
3 pots *Ceratopteris thalictroides*
3 bunches *Hydrocotyle leucocephala*

✔ For the middleground:
1 pot *Echinodorus cordifolius*
2 bunches *Hygrophila corymbosa*
3 bunches *Rotala rotundifolia*
1 plant *Nymphaea lotus*
*3 pots (or plants) *Cryptocoryne crispatula* var. *balansae*
1 plant *Echinodorus bleheri*

✔ For the foreground:
5 plants *Echinodorus quadricostatus*
*3 pots (or plants) *Cryptocoryne wendtii*
*2 pots *Cryptocoryne nevillii*

Planting diagram of the sample community aquarium described below left.

*5 pots *Lobelia cardinalis*
*3 pots *Anubias barteri* var. *nana*
*Note: If these plants are potted, remove the mineral wool before planting in your aquarium.

"Beginner's" Aquarium (60 × 30 × 30 cm) (24 × 12 × 12 inches)

The right layout is especially important in a small tank because the smaller the volume, the greater the fluctuations in water quality. Try to provide dense plant cover with a large proportion of fast-growing species. This prevents excessive growth of algae and helps keep water quality nearly constant.

Sample plant layout (20 plants):

3 bunches *Limnophila sessiliflora*
5 plants *Vallisneria asiatica*
1 bunch *Ludwigia palustris* × *L. repens*
1 plant *Echinodorus amazonicus*
2 pots (or a clump) *Cryptocoryne wendtii*
1 pot (or a clump) *Cryptocoryne* × *willisii*
1 bunch *Alternanthera reineckii* 'Rosaefolia'
3 pots *Micranthemum umbrosum*
3 pots (or clumps) *Sagittaria subulata*

Schooling Fish Aquarium

An aquarium with one or more groups of schooling fish like Neon Tetras or Harlequin Rasboras should offer plenty of open swimming room—at least in the front half of the tank. Taller plants should be confined to the background.

Background: *Vallisneria spiralis, Alternanthera sessilis, Hydrocotyle leucocephala, Ceratopteris thalictroides, Hygrophila polysperma, Limnophila sessiliflora.*
Middleground: *Cryptocoryne crispatula* var. *balansae, C. beckettii, Sagittaria platyphylla, Lobelia cardinalis, Micranthemum umbrosum, Microsorium pteropus.*
Foreground: *Anubias barteri* var. *nana, Cryptocoryne wendtii, Cladophora aegagropila, Lilaeopsis novae-zelandiae, Sagittaria subulata.*

Discus Aquarium

Since Discus require relatively warm water (around 28°C [82°F]), the choice of suitable plants is limited to a few species. Plants with floating leaves provide shady spots.

Background: *Hygrophila polysperma, H. salicifolia, Hydrocotyle leucocephala, Vallisneria spiralis, V. asiatica.*
Middleground: *Echinodorus bleheri, E. martii, E. schlüteri, E. cordifolius, E. amazonicus, E. horizontalis, E. parviflorus, Alternanthera reineckii* 'Rosaefolia', *Mayaca fluviatilis, Hygrophila corymbosa.*
Foreground: *Echinodorus quadricostatus, E. tenellus, E. bolivianus, Sagittaria subulata.*

Cichlid Tank

Some cichlids, such as those from Africa's Rift Lakes, must be kept in hard water, and moreover they like to eat the vegetation. Only a few plants can thrive under such conditions.

Background: *Anubias congensis, A. lanceolata, Cryptocoryne aponogetifolia, Sagittaria subulata.*
Middleground: *Anubias barteri* var. *barteri, A. gracilis, A. heterophylla, Microsorium pteropus.*
Foreground: *Anubias barteri* var. *nana, A. afzellii.*

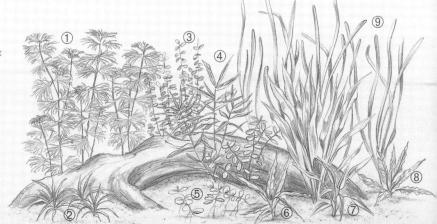

Beginner's Aquarium:
1 Limnophila sessiliflora,
2 Sagittaria subulata,
3 Ludwigia palustris ×
L. repens,
4 Alternanthera reineckii 'Rosaefolia',
5 Micranthemum umbrosum,
6 Cryptocoryne wendtii,
7 C. willisii,
8 Echinodorus amazonicus,
9 Vallisneria spiralis.

AQUARIUM EQUIPMENT AND WATER QUALITY

In order to avoid aggravation or unpleasant surprises and be able to provide their pets with the most natural habitat possible, even dedicated plant lovers should give at least a little thought to aquarium equipment and water chemistry.

The Right Location

Proper technique begins with the correct choice and preparation of a site:

✔ The aquarium should never be exposed to direct sun. Because of the danger of overheating, it should not be placed in front of a radiator, either.

✔ If you are not using a special aquarium stand, you must set the tank on a sturdy, perfectly level surface. Placing a special aquarium pad made of sponge rubber (from the pet store) or a sheet of styrofoam beneath the tank has proven to be very helpful here.

✔ The connections for electricity (large tanks require several outlets) and water should be as close to the tank as possible.

Caution: A tank only 120 cm (48 inches) in length weighs about 300 kg (660 pounds) when filled. For this reason, the base and the floor on which it stands must be extremely sturdy. When in doubt, especially in older buildings, you should have the load-bearing capacity of the floor checked by an expert.

There's always something new to discover when contemplating this beautiful underwater landscape.

All-Glass Aquariums

The round goldfish bowl has had its day. Pet stores today carry aquariums in almost every size and shape. They are made of individual panes of crystal- or float-glass glued together with silicone sealant.

Safety first: Glass aquariums must be very sturdily built. *Manufacturers are required to comply with strict regulations.* For example, the glass must be 4 to 5 mm (0.16 to 0.2 inch) thick for an aquarium 60 cm (24 inches) long, and 8 to 10 mm (0.3 to 0.4 inch) thick for an aquarium 120 cm (48 inches) long. The static load-bearing capacity of these tanks is about five times greater than would be necessary because of the water pressure.

Complete aquarium setups: Aquariums with the standard dimensions of 60 × 30 × 30 cm (24 × 12 × 12 inches) hold only 50 liters (13 gallons) of water. They are primarily sold in pet stores as part of so-called complete setups. They spare the beginner the difficult task of assembling the individual components of an aquarium. It's a practical, thrifty solution, but unfortunately one that is often followed by disappointment. This is because the smaller an aquarium, the more the water quality fluctu-

TIP

Safety Around the Aquarium

Water and electricity are a dangerous combination, and water damage caused by a leaky aquarium can run into quite a bit of money. Try to minimize the risks:

✔ *Buy only equipment bearing the UL listing mark.*

✔ Use a ground-fault circuit interrupter, or GFCI (available in electrical supply stores as well as many pet stores), which protects you from electrical shock in the event of a malfunction.

✔ With large aquariums and increased current demand for lights, filters, and heaters, you should distribute the individual devices among several outlets.

✔ Always unplug aquarium equipment before you work on it.

✔ Don't attempt to repair any electrical components of these devices yourself. This is best left to professionals.

✔ Have coverage for water damage due to a leaky aquarium included in your homeowners' insurance.

ates and the more unfavorable the conditions are for plants and fish (→ Tip, page 35). Also, importantly, the strip light sold with them produces inadequate light for the growth of most plants.

Small aquariums are commonly assumed to require less care, but in fact their water quality must be checked more frequently because dangerous situations can arise much more quickly in them. Problems with algae (→ page 55), poor plant growth, and fish diseases also occur much more often.

Choose the largest possible tank: The most popular standard aquarium is 100 cm (40 inches) long, 40 cm (16 inches) wide, and 50 cm (20 inches) high. It holds about 200 liters (52 gallons) of water, a volume that not only offers many different possibilities for stocking and planting (→ HOW-TO, pages 26/27), but also is more forgiving of various mistakes in maintenance. For this reason, beginners in particular should select the largest tank possible.

Aquariums in all shapes: In addition to the standard rectangular aquarium, there are very decorative panorama tanks with angled fronts, pentagonal aquariums for optimal use of a corner location, and bow-front models. If you have something special in mind, you can also have an aquarium made to order in almost any size. Just remember that a planted tank should be no more than 60 cm (24 inches) high. Otherwise, lighting will be difficult and your choice of plants will be definitely limited.

Aquarium Lighting

One of the most important factors for plant growth is light, and the variety of lighting options offered by pet stores is correspondingly wide. Which lights you should consider depends on the type of aquarium: Is the top of the tank open or closed? Both styles have advantages and disadvantages.

Open aquariums do not have a cover and are usually illuminated by lights hanging from the ceiling. Plants emerging from the water or floating on the surface are clearly visible, and it is easier to work in the tank when doing maintenance chores. However, much more water evaporates from an open aquarium, and there is an increased chance of fish jumping out.

✔ Increased humidity can sometimes lead to the formation of mold and mildew on cooler outside walls or behind cabinets.

✔ As water evaporates, all the minerals, waste

products, and dissolved salts responsible for water hardness remain behind in the aquarium and accumulate there as time goes by. The only way for you to counteract this is by replacing evaporated water exclusively with distilled water—and that is a very expensive proposition. This is one reason why it is essential to perform weekly 10%–20% partial water changes.

With closed aquariums the lights are in a housing mounted on top of the tank. This aquarium hood is usually made of plastic sides and panels and effectively prevents the evaporation of water. In addition, it acts as an optical boundary to the underwater landscape, which then seems to be illuminated from within.

Metal vapor lamps: Pendant lighting fixtures for open-top aquariums are usually equipped with mercury vapor lamps or metal halide lamps. While they provide concentrated light for the aquarium, they illuminate only a very small area. As a rule of thumb, one mercury vapor lamp is enough for an aquarium up to 60 cm (24 inches) in length maximum. On the other hand, metal vapor lamps are very bright and ensure that sufficient light for growth reaches the bottom even with extremely deep tanks (water depth over 60 cm [24 inches]).

Fluorescent tubes: Both open-top as well as closed aquariums can be illuminated more evenly with fluorescent tubes. They come in a variety of lengths and in many power ratings from 4 to 58 watts. With fluorescent tubes, it is possible to provide the right intensity of illumination for almost any size aquarium. How much light an aquarium needs is a matter of disagreement among experts. As a rule of

Along with lights, filter, and water heater, an undergravel heater is a useful addition to the aquarium equipment.

thumb, you should allow 0.3 to 0.5 watts per liter (1 to 2 watts per gallon) of water. That is enough for rapid growth of light-hungry plants, but does not put the more shade-loving species under stress.

All light is not the same: Fluorescent tubes are available in different light colors. For example, there are special models which enhance the colors of fish. For good plant growth you should use at least some special plant bulbs with a proportionately high output of red and

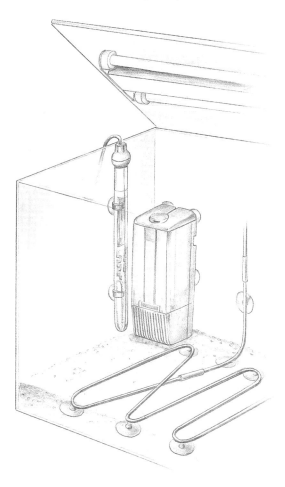

Typical Malawi cichlid tank with carved rocks planted with anubias.

blue light. If you combine these with tubes designed to simulate the spectrum of sunlight, the colors will look especially natural.

VHO (very high output) fluorescent fixtures are recommended for deep aquariums (over 12″), and produce a much greater amount of lumens per watt.

Save energy: Fluorescent tubes give off very little heat. For example, for every watt used, you get about 20 percent more light with them than with mercury vapor lamps and many times more than with tungsten bulbs. Placing special aluminum reflectors behind the bulbs can increase the light output by as much as 25 percent. Energy-saving high output fluorescent tubes allow luxuriant plant growth in water up to a depth of 60 cm (24 inches).

Controlling equipment with timers: Aquarium lighting is usually regulated with a timer. The optimum duration of lighting for aquarium plants is 10 to 12 hours a day.

Caution: Drastically reducing the period of exposure to light when algae appear does not solve the problem—on the contrary, it severely retards the growth of higher plants. Lighting durations of more than 12 hours almost exclusively foster the growth of unwelcome algae, as well.

Twilight in the aquarium: Fluorescent tubes can also be slowly brightened or dimmed if you use a special electronic ballast equipped with digital control (from the pet store). This way you can simulate natural sunrise and sunset as well as pale moonlight. This is a major step towards creating the most naturalistic conditions possible in the aquarium. Gradually adjusting the light intensity gives your plants and fish the time they need to switch from nighttime to daytime metabolism and back again. For you as the observer, these periods of low light reveal a whole new world in the aquarium.

Note: Lighting is probably the single most important factor in establishing an aquarium. There are many excellent aquarium lights designed specifically for your aquarium available in your local pet store.

Heating Systems

Several options are available for heating tropical aquariums.

<u>Aquarium heater/thermostats</u> are electrical heating coils encased in sturdy glass tubes and attached to the back wall of the tank with suction cups. They have a built-in thermostat which can be used to set the desired temperature. How powerful a heater/thermostat has to be depends on the volume of water in the tank and the temperature of the surrounding area. For an aquarium located in a living area, figure on about one watt per liter (4 watts per gallon) of aquarium water.

<u>Thermofilters</u> have an electrical heater built into the filter canister that works like a continuous-flow water heater. Here, too, water temperature is regulated by a thermostat.

<u>Undergravel heaters:</u> In addition to adjusting the temperature of the open water in the aquarium with a heater/thermostat or thermofilter, it has proved beneficial to heat the

substrate as well. This is accomplished using electrical heating cables which are attached to the glass bottom of the tank by means of special cable anchors and suction cups and then covered completely with gravel or sand.

Important: Only in rare cases (high room temperature, lights which give off a great deal of heat) can an aquarium be heated by an undergravel heater alone. The substrate should be a maximum of 1 to 2°C (2 to 4°F) warmer than the open aquarium water. Too much heat has an adverse effect on plant growth.

<u>Modern aquarium heating systems</u> monitor the temperature of the water and substrate and establish an optimum thermal gradient in the aquarium. In tropical community tanks (disregarding special aquarium types) the water temperature should be set at about 26°C (79°F). The optimum substrate temperature would then be 27°C (81°F). The temperature difference in the aquarium creates weak convection currents which circulate through the substrate (→ illustration, page 34).

Cardamine lyrata is effective because of its platelike leaves on thin petioles.

Lowering the temperature at night: Temperature is one of the most important environmental factors in the aquarium. The warmer the water and substrate, the more oxygen fish, microorganisms, and plants will consume. At night, therefore, while the plants are not photosynthesizing and so are not producing any oxygen, the temperature should be lowered a bit, just as usually happens in nature. This nocturnal drop results in more compact plant growth, and many ornamental fish breeders claim that it also makes the fish less susceptible to disease.

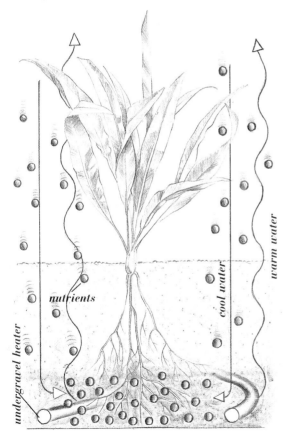

nutrients

undergravel heater

cool water

warm water

Filtration

In all freshwater aquariums, ornamental fish are kept at much higher population densities than they occur in the wild. If you wanted to follow nature's guidelines, you would only be able to keep one or two fish at most in a 100-liter (26-gallon) tank. In practice, though, this would hardly be enough to satisfy most aquarists. As it is, the waste products from so many fish pollute the water and must be removed by means of filters.

Filter systems:
✔ Internal filters operate inside the aquarium and are usually attached to the glass with suction cups. They are easy to install and need no connecting hose. Because of their relatively low filtration volume, they are generally used only for aquariums up to 200 liters (52 gallons).
✔ External filters have the advantage of a much higher filtration volume and consequently a longer service life (the period of time between two filter cleanings) as well as greater flexibility with regard to filter media.

Important: When choosing a filter, you should ask your pet dealer for detailed advice. As a rule, filtration volume cannot be too large. It is important, though, that the output of the filter pump be adequate for the size of the aquarium so that water will circulate throughout the entire tank.

Filtration stages: In filtration itself, two stages are differentiated:
✔ Mechanical filtration: Particles of dirt are trapped in materials like synthetic foam, polyfiber pads, or filter floss.

The temperature difference between the heated substrate and the water allows nutrients to seep into the substrate.

✔ Biological filtration: Toxic substances are transformed into harmless compounds by bacteria which colonize the filter media (→ illustration, page 38).

Special filter media can be used in external filters:

✔ *Activated carbon adsorbs contaminants* such as metals, dyes, and toxins.

✔ Special exchange resins remove dissolved substances by chemical and physical means.

✔ Peat granules act as mechanical and biological filters and also lower the pH and soften the water.

Carbon Dioxide Fertilization

In terms of dry mass, plants are more than 40 percent carbon, and the only form in which they can take up this element is carbon dioxide (CO_2). In addition to light, temperature, and nutrient supply, the level of dissolved carbon dioxide in the water is the fourth important environmental factor for good plant growth.

No plant growth without carbon dioxide: Absorption of carbon dioxide occurs as part of an extremely complicated process called photosynthesis, in which plants utilize the energy of light in order to transform carbon dioxide and water into oxygen and carbohydrates. These carbohydrates are stored or used in making plant tissue. The oxygen is released into the water, where it is available to all living things for respiration.

Pros and cons of carbon dioxide fertilization: The question remains of whether there is enough carbon dioxide available in the water for luxuriant plant growth, or if it is necessary to provide it as supplemental fertilizer. This is one of the most hotly debated topics among aquarists.

✔ Arguments in favor of supplemental carbon dioxide fertilization include better provision of plants with carbon and the ability to adjust the

TIP

Stable Environmental Conditions

Rarely are all environmental factors in the aquarium ideal, because the interrelations among the individual organisms are too complex and their requirements are too diverse. Yet aquarium plants can thrive even under supposedly unfavorable conditions. The secret lies in the stability of the environmental factors.

Adjustment takes time: Give your plants enough time to get used to the light, temperature, and water conditions that you can provide for them. Don't keep fiddling around with the various factors —most plants are quite capable of adapting, if you just let them.

Stability is also a question of size: The smaller the aquarium, the more the water conditions will fluctuate and the worse the living conditions for fish and plants will be. Keeping a 60-liter (15-gallon) tank "beginner's" aquarium biologically stable for any length of time is a challenge even for an experienced aquarist. For this reason, it is better to choose a tank that is too big rather than one that is too small.

pH of the water by adding carbon dioxide (→ page 37).

✔ Opponents of carbon dioxide fertilization argue that there is always more than enough carbon dioxide available due to gas exchange at the water surface and most of all to the respiration of fish, plants, and microorganisms.

In practice, of course, the special conditions in an aquarium must always be taken into consideration. In general, however, the more heavily planted an aquarium, the more it makes sense to fertilize with carbon dioxide, since larger amounts of it are extracted from the water than are made available by respiration and gas exchange. This becomes evident when the pH value rises above 8.0 or calcium deposits appear on the leaves (→ page 38).

Carbon dioxide fertilization equipment: Various fertilization systems are available in pet stores. They usually consist of a carbon dioxide cylinder with pressure reducer, a needle valve for regulating the flow, and a reactor which is installed in the aquarium and where the gas is dissolved in water. Elaborate and correspondingly expensive systems have convenient control mechanisms which make it easier to monitor carbon dioxide injection into the aquarium water.

Water Quality in the Aquarium

The quality of aquarium water for plants and fish depends primarily on the presence of dissolved substances which are interrelated in many different ways. Pet stores offer measuring instruments or test kits suitable for determining the concentrations at which the individual substances are present; these range from convenient but expensive electronic monitors to small chemistry kits with various reagents to test strips that need only be dipped briefly into the water and then turn a characteristic color. Many stores also offer to perform extensive water analyses.

Carbonate Hardness, pH, and Carbon Dioxide

These three water quality parameters are directly related to each other.

Carbon dioxide level influences the pH: Free carbon dioxide dissolved in water is a weak acid (carbonic acid) and lowers the pH—the more dissolved CO_2, the more acidic the water becomes. How much free carbon dioxide there is in your aquarium depends basically on three factors.

✔ All respiratory processes release carbon dioxide into the water.

✔ Growing plants, on the other hand, absorb carbon dioxide and bind it.

✔ Carbonate hardness of the water (measured in degrees German carbonate hardness, °dKH) also binds carbon dioxide.

The higher (more alkaline) this value, the

The dark green leaf color of Dwarf Anubias contrasts with the brown of the root.

lower the level of free carbon dioxide and the higher the pH.

Good conditions for plants: For optimum plant growth, you should try to maintain a pH between 6.5 and 7.5 with a carbonate hardness of 6 to 10 °dKH in your aquarium.

Note: Some fish require hard, alkaline water, and this severely limits the variety of plants you can use.

✔ If the pH rises, most nutrients will be present as insoluble compounds. This has a particularly significant impact on trace elements (→ page 39). While they are still present in sufficient quantities, they can no longer be absorbed by the plants. This is called nutrient fixation.

Photo left: Water Sprite, **Ceratopteris thalictroides.**
Photo right: Dwarf Rotala, **Rotala rotundifolia.**

✔ Excessively high carbonate hardness has a direct adverse effect on plant growth, since under these conditions only a small amount of free carbon dioxide remains available for photosynthesis.

Influencing pH: Problems usually arise in the aquarium as a result of excessively hard water and the high pH associated with it. But you don't have to put up with pH values that are less than ideal:

✔ By reducing carbonate hardness (for example by mixing in soft water or using a pH-lowering preparation from the pet store) carbon dioxide is released and the pH drops.
✔ Carbon dioxide fertilization also lowers the pH.

Tip: Some plant species (for instance members of the genera *Vallisneria* and *Elodea*) are able to extract carbon dioxide from hydrogen carbonates. As a result, they develop hard, transparent calcium deposits on their leaves, which then tend to be colonized by special algae. In this case, you should test the water quality and take steps to correct the problem as soon as possible (→ page 55).

Nitrogen Compounds

Metabolic products and uneaten food load the water with nitrogen compounds. These can be strong poisons or plant nutrients.

Ammonium and ammonia: Ammonium (NH_4^+), in addition to nitrate, is the compound in which plants can take up nitrogen. Certain microorganisms convert ammonium to nitrite and then to nitrate. At first, a high level of ammonium in the water appears to pose no problem. But as the pH rises, more and more of the ammonium changes to ammonia (NH_3), which is extremely toxic for fish. When the ammonium level exceeds 0.1 mg/l (0.1 ppm) and the pH is above 7.5, you must carry out a water change immediately. This danger is especially great in a newly set-up aquarium. Once it is broken in, high levels of ammonium almost never recur.

Nitrite (NO_2^+) is also very toxic for fish and should not be present at detectable levels in the aquarium. As a rule, it is produced only as a transient intermediate during the conversion of ammonium into nitrate (→ illustration, left). The bacteria which carry out this process are concentrated in the filter and in the substrate.

Nitrate (NO_3^+) is the final product of nitrogen degradation. Plants absorb this essential nutrient throught their leaves and roots, purifying the

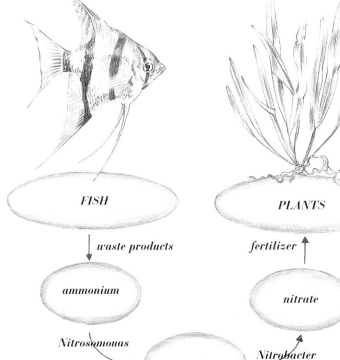

FISH

waste products

ammonium

Nitrosomonas

nitrite

PLANTS

fertilizer

nitrate

Nitrobacter

Fish, bacteria, and plants are involved in the nitrogen cycle.

water in the process—next to the production of oxygen, their most important task in the aquarium.

Phosphate

Phosphorus in the form of phosphate (PO_4^{3+}) is another of the major nutrients, or "macronutrients," required by all plants. Normally it is plentiful in the aquarium. Sometimes it is even too plentiful, and this can lead to the proliferation of algae and nonspecific growth disturbances. High phosphate levels in excess of 2 mg/l (2 ppm) can result from over-feeding or from large quantities of decaying biomass, such as occurs after the use of a molluscicide (→ page 56). Phosphate can also accumulate in the aquarium if the undergravel heater raises the substrate temperature too high, killing most of the plant roots.

Potassium, Magnesium, Calcium

These three minerals are also major nutrients. While magnesium and calcium are usually present in sufficient amounts in most aquariums, potassium is often lacking.

Potassium is crucial for tissue rigidity and root growth—a deficiency can be recognized by the generally droopy condition of the plant. Regular administration of special potassium fertilizers, available from the pet store, will remedy the situation.

Trace Elements

A number of nutrients are indeed essential for plant growth, but they are only required in very small amounts. These include iron and manganese. Deficiencies rarely occur in a mature aquarium where the pH is not too high (→ Fertilization, page 51).

CARE DURING VACATION

Aquarium plants themselves need no special provisions. Avoid excessive fertilization and postpone any maintenance on the plants until you return from vacation. Aside from that, keep in mind the following:

✔ *Check to make sure that all technical equipment is functioning properly.*

✔ *Clean your filter about a week before you go on vacation and carry out a substantial partial water change (about one third of the water).*

✔ *Depending on your fish stock and the length of time you will be away, it may make sense to use an automatic feeder. Just be sure to test this device for a while beforehand so you can determine the correct daily food quantities.*

✔ *If you want to entrust someone else with the feeding of your fish, you should give that person detailed instructions. Try to prevent the well-intentioned overfeeding of your fish and resultant contamination of the water with waste products, which are all too common in such cases.*

SETTING UP AND PLANTING THE AQUARIUM

What aquarist wouldn't want to have a lush underwater jungle as a habitat for tropical fish and a decorative addition to the living room? When setting up a new aquarium and designing the habitat, you can give free rein to your imagination.

The Right Substrate

The structure of the substrate is of crucial importance for long-term plant growth as well as for subsequent functioning of the aquarium.

The right particle size: Many aquarists use either very coarse or very fine gravel. Yet healthy substrate conditions cannot develop in materials like these—after the plants are put in, they often fail to thrive or even die off altogether. The ideal gravel has a particle size of 2 to 4 mm (about 1/8 inch).

Put in the right substrate:

✔ As a plant lover, you should give some thought to an undergravel heating system (→ page 33), which creates particularly good growing conditions. It is laid down directly on the bottom of the tank.

✔ Next comes the nutrient layer: it is 1 to 2 cm (1/2 to 1 inch) deep and consists of aquarium gravel mixed with a special substrate material such as laterite and possibly an aquarium

plant fertilizer (from the pet store). These mixtures are rich in clay minerals that can bind plant nutrients and store them so they do not contaminate the water. Aquarium plants can then draw on this nutrient reserve as needed.

✔ Last comes a top covering of at least 4 cm (1½ inches) of washed gravel.

Functions of the substrate: The nutrient layer and top covering together make up the substrate, which should be at least 6 cm (2½ inches), or better yet 8 cm (3 inches), deep. It becomes a habitat for microorganisms which break down the waste products in the aquarium and thus purify the water. In addition, it represents a store of nutrients for the aquarium plants, but one which is not available to aquatic algae inhabiting the tank.

Arranging the substrate: The substrate of your aquarium does not have to be level. If you want to make your tank seem deeper, it's a good idea to have the top layer slope gently upward from the front to the back of the tank. You can also construct actual terraces (→ illustration, page 43) which divide up the aquarium in an interesting way and create different levels for planting.

The different colors and shapes of these cryptocorynes give this aquascape its charm.

PROPER CARE OF AQUARIUM PLANTS

An underwater garden needs care: Only with regular pruning and rejuvenation, a balanced nutrient supply, optimal lighting, and stable water conditions will a thriving plant community be able to develop.

The Aquarium—a Dynamic Habitat

The aquarium with its plants, fish, roots, rocks, and open areas form a closed environment, but one which is subject to its own dynamics and so undergoes constant change. Fish reproduce, get bigger, and age. Plants grow and spread. Water quality can change simply as a result of evaporation and refilling, but also because of the many biological and chemical processes that occur in it. Thus the impression that the observer has of an aquarium is only a snapshot of this ever-changing microcosm. This is especially true of the flora.

Competition among plants: Plants are constantly competing with each other for room, nutrients, and light. Since an aquarium is, after all, a limited space, humans must intervene to monitor and care for it, otherwise the tank would become completely overgrown in time.

A group of Red Hygrophila contrasts sharply with the green background.

Apart from the fact that there would no longer be enough open swimming room for the fish, competition would also take its toll on diversity. In the end, only a few plant species would survive.

An underwater garden needs care: A beautiful aquarium is like a miniature garden in which natural growth is guided along aesthetic paths. Open areas are kept clear of colonizing species, and thickets which have grown too large are cut back. The spread of plants that reproduce too freely must be checked (→ illustration, page 50). Old plants should be rejuvenated regularly and diseased ones should be replaced. In order for the plants to grow well enough that you can use them to create an attractive underwater garden, they must be supplied regularly with nutrients in the form of fertilizers developed specially for the aquarium.

You will find all of these plant care measures described in greater detail on the following pages. There—as in the portrait section (→ pages 13–25)—a basic distinction will be made between rosette and stem plants.

Propagation, Rejuvenation, and Pruning

Sexual propagation by means of seeds plays practically no role in aquarium plants, since only a few species can bloom in the tank. Asexual propagation, on the other hand, is extremely important for the care and rejuvenation of the aquarium landscape. Here we can differentiate the following methods:

✔ Runners or offsets,
✔ Adventitious plantlets,
✔ Division of the rootstock or rhizome, and
✔ Cuttings.

Rosette Plants

Rosette plants require very little care. It's enough to remove old leaves and thin out the stands now and then. The plants reproduce by forming different types of "daughter plants" depending on the species:

Runners are side shoots on whose ends new plants develop. They occur, for example, in the genus *Vallisneria* (→ page 18). Many runners are only a few millimeters (a fraction of an inch) long, others grow to 20 cm (8 inches). You can limit their spread with scissors.

Adventitious plantlets develop on the flowering stems of the larger *Echinodorus* species (→ page 15), for instance, or on the leaves of *Microsorium pteropus* (→ page 24). They can be detached and planted.

Division of the rootstock: Other species like *Anubias barteri* (→ page 14) reproduce by means of thickened rootstocks, or rhizomes, along which new plants arise. These, too, can be detached.

Stem Plants

The primary type of care required by stem plants is pruning. Selective trimming keeps the plants from growing too tall and encourages bushier growth. Growing tips or side shoots can also be taken as cuttings. Insert the cutting in the substrate up to the lowest node after removing all leaves from this area—otherwise they will rot.

Most rosette plants form runners which creep along the bottom.

Maintenance Schedule for Aquarium Plants

Daily Care	✔ Check plants for injuries or signs of feeding damage. ✔ Is the water temperature correct? Are the electrical devices working properly?
Weekly Care	✔ Check pH and change up to one fifth of the water as needed. ✔ Siphon up the mulm from the substrate (→ HOW-TO Plant Care, pages 58/59). ✔ Clean aquarium glass. ✔ Remove dead or damaged leaves. ✔ Add supplemental complete fertilizer.
Monthly Care	✔ Take steps to control the spread of plants. ✔ Prune stem plants as needed. ✔ Change up to one third of the water; replenish with soft water if required. ✔ Clean internal filter if present.
Annual Care	✔ Replace fluorescent tubes (→ page 55). ✔ Replenish slow-release fertilizer with substrate fertilizer balls (→ page 51).
Care as Needed	✔ Replace plant groups that are growing poorly. ✔ Clean external filter as soon as there is a noticeable decrease in flow rate.

Fertilization

In addition to light, carbon dioxide, and water, aquarium plants need a whole series of "nutrients" in the form of water-soluble salts to synthesize plant tissue. These nutrients are either produced naturally through the breakdown of organic substances or must be supplied from the outside as fertilizer. Keep in mind: A thriving plant community resulting from optimal nutrient supply is not only a delight to the eye, but it benefits the entire underwater environment in the aquarium as well. In fertilization, a distinction is made between the initial provision of essential nutrients and the regular supplemental fertilization which occurs later.

Providing Essential Nutrients

Substrate fertilization (→ page 41) is the simplest and most effective method of supplying plants with essential nutrients. Pet stores offer a wide variety of substrate mixtures, fertilizer granules, and so-called initial sticks. Ask your dealer for advice on which products are best for your aquarium.

Caution: Do not use pure peat plates in the substrate. They have not proven successful. Because they release large amounts of humic acid, excessively acidic conditions develop, resulting in the death of most plant roots over time.

Regular Supplemental Fertilization

Pet stores offer various preparations for routine supplemental fertilization or for specific treatment of nutrient deficiencies:

✔ Liquid fertilizers are practical and easy to use. Regular addition of small amounts of fertilizer using an automatic dosing device is ideal for plant growth.

✔ Fertilizer balls are an excellent way to provide supplemental fertilizer to individual plants (e.g., *Echinodorus bleheri*, → page 15). They are composed of clay particles loaded with nutrients and are pressed into the substrate around the plants to be fertilized.

Generally speaking, it is best to fertilize often, but at lower doses. This way, you will be providing a constant supply of nutrients, which the plants will appreciate (→ Tip, page 35).

Ammania gracilis needs relatively bright light and a good supply of nutrients.

Complete fertilizers: Fertilizers designed especially for use in the aquarium are usually so-called complete fertilizers; that means they supply all the essential nutrients. Nitrogen compounds and phosphates, which are a major component of garden fertilizers, are avoided as much as possible in products for the aquarium, since these nutrients are usually present in abundance (→ pages 38/39).

Trace elements: Trace elements like iron, manganese, copper, or molybdenum play an import role in the nutrition of aquarium plants. The plants need only tiny amounts of these elements—just traces, in fact—but they absolutely

must have them. If just one is missing, or if it is not readily available for the plant, then growth is severely restricted.

Iron and manganese deficiency: In the aquarium, two trace element deficiencies occur most often. Both lead to yellowing of the leaves, known as chlorosis:
✔ Iron deficiency is characterized by leaves and leaf veins turning pale yellow.
✔ With manganese deficiency, the leaves turn yellow, but the veins stay green.

Often these two deficiency diseases are associated: Since iron deficiency is a common problem, many aquarists regularly add iron fertilizer to the aquarium as a preventive measure. Manganese, however, is very similar to iron—plants absorb both elements by the same biological

Exotic growth forms: Crystalwort (front), Lake Ball (rear).

mechanisms. Excess iron in the water can therefore occupy all the plant's transport pathways and thus inhibit the uptake of manganese or even prevent it entirely.

The influence of pH: The pH value or degree of acidity of the water directly influences the availability of nutrients for the plants (→ page 37). Most of these nutrients can best be absorbed by the plants in slightly acidic water (pH 6.5). In the alkaline range on the other hand (pH above 7.5), nutrient uptake becomes increasingly difficult.

Troubleshooting

Problems	Cause	Remedy
Leaves and veins turn pale yellow, then glassy, and finally die.	Iron deficiency	Add iron fertilizer and adjust water values if pH is above 7.5.
Leaves turn yellow, but veins remain green.	Manganese deficiency, often as a result of over-fertilization with iron	Change up to one third of the water and add trace element fertilizer.
Shoots of stem plants keep getting longer and thinner—overall growth stagnates.	Insufficient light	Replace fluorescent tubes, install shiny reflectors or provide more light for the aquarium.
Leaves display round holes, leaf edges appear nibbled.	Snail damage	Introduce snail-eating fish or use a molluscicide (→ page 56).
Leaves display large ragged holes, leaf veins are often exposed.	Damage caused by algae-eating catfish	Provide fish with plenty of green food (food tablets).
Substrate has black areas, foul-smelling gas bubbles arise, plants rot away.	Compacted substrate: incorrect substrate with too much organic material was used.	Replace substrate and set up again correctly (→ page 41); use of an undergravel heater is best.

Damage to Plants

Despite all their flexibility when faced with adverse environmental conditions, aquatic plants can get sick. Only rarely are problems in the aquarium due to bacteria or viruses. Most damage to plants is a result of poor water quality and improper or insufficient lighting—conditions which the competing algae often cope with better. In addition, some aquarium animals like to eat the vegetation. Observe your plants carefully and respond quickly at the first signs of damage or disturbances of growth.

Poor Growth Factors

If the plants stop growing, change color, or develop holes, this usually indicates that something is wrong with the water quality.

✔ If the pH and water hardness are high, it is more difficult to supply plants with the nutrients they need (→ page 37), which can lead to stunted growth. A hard deposit of calcium on the leaves is a consequence of such poor water quality and the associated lack of free carbon dioxide (→ page 35).

✔ A deficiency or excess of nutrients and trace elements can both be almost disastrous for the plants.

Clean up the water: Unfortunately, it is difficult for the layperson to differentiate individual deficiency symptoms and therefore difficult to ascribe the problem to a specific nutrient deficiency. Often the only thing that helps here is a thorough clean-up of the water. Carry out a major water change (up to one third of the volume) and repeat the procedure one week later. At the same time, add a good complete aquarium fertilizer containing the full spectrum of trace nutrients in addition to the major nutrients.

Important: It is advisable to check the most important water parameters regularly so that you can react at the first signs of any trouble.

Insufficient light: The situation is similar for growth disturbances resulting from too little light. If plants had been doing well previously, the cause is usually a decrease in the output of the fluorescent tubes. If plants have never thrived, the cause is probably inadequate light fixtures. They should be replaced by new tubes after about a year at most. More than one aquarist has been surprised by the remarkable effect this simple measure has on plant growth.

Important: Never change all the tubes at once, but rather do it gradually after a period of two to three weeks. Otherwise, only the fast-growing algae will benefit initially from the sudden increase in light. The higher plants need a few days to adjust to the new situation and take full advantage of it.

Success takes time: Once you get the water conditions back in order and optimize the lighting, the plants will begin to grow again. Depending on the plant species, this can take a few days. Don't be impatient. You can recognize healthy new growth by the deep green heart leaves—this is what the youngest leaves in the center of rosette plants are called—and by the fresh growing tips.

Algal Growth

You cannot safeguard against algal spores. They are everywhere, and once they have proliferated, it is difficult to get the better of them. They not only compete with aquarium plants, they can actually overgrow them.

✔ Provide optimal and above all stable growing conditions (→ Tip, page 35) for your plants, and you will

Ramshorn snails and algae-eating catfish damage aquarium plants.

find yourself halfway along the road to a nearly algae-free aquarium.

✔ A number of tropical fish are efficient algae eaters. These include such popular species as Siamese Flying Foxes and Suckermouth Catfish. Find out which of these fish your pet dealer carries and ask his advice.

Algicides: If you are still troubled by algal blooms, sometimes the only thing left for you to do is use an algicide. Keep in mind, though, that such preparations always harm the higher aquarium plants to some extent as well. For this reason, they are not generally recommended, but if used, it is especially important to follow the manufacturer's instructions precisely. After treatment with an algicide, you should provide good growing conditions as soon as possible (→ page 55).

It's also a good idea to add some groups of fast-growing plants to your plant community (→ Plants in Portrait, pages 13–25).

Feeding Damage

In the aquarium, two groups of animals can do serious damage to the plants (→ illustration, page 55).

Snail damage can be recognized by round holes in leaves and gnawed leaf edges. A massive outbreak can quickly decimate your plant community. But it is possible to safeguard against this:

✔ Introduce snail-eating fish like Clown Loaches or Pufferfish.

✔ The pet store carries effective molluscicides. Bear in mind, though, that most contain copper salts that may harm the plants and that the sudden demise of many snails can foul the water.

Some species of catfish like to graze on the very fine coating of algae which grows on leaves, and in the process they damage the outermost layer of the leaf. As a result of this injury, the underlying tissue dies. Characteristic of such feeding damage are skeletonized leaves with only the leaf veins remaining. You can counteract this activity, most of which is nocturnal, by feeding your fish more—ideally in the form of tablet foods with a high proportion of plant matter in the mixture.

Star Rotala (**Eustralis stellata**) *is one of the more demanding species.*

10 Golden Rules
for Proper Plant Care

1 Aquarium plants are more adaptable than is generally believed, but they need time to adjust to a new environment.

2 An aquarium can only function when the most important demands of the plant and animal species are compatible.

3 Once a month, check the pH and carbonate hardness. If there is a problem with these values, you should change up to one third of the water.

4 Fast-growing plants need more care than slow-growing species, but contribute more to the biological equilibrium of your aquarium.

5 Never consider a single environmental factor independently of the others. It takes light, temperature, and available nutrient supply all working together to produce healthy, luxuriant plant growth.

6 A properly functioning aquarium with thriving plants is your best defense against excessive algal growth.

7 It's better to fertilize your aquarium plants often but in smaller doses. This is more effective and contaminates the water less.

8 Clean only the surface of the aquarium substrate—up to a maximum depth of (2½ inches) 1 cm.

9 Remove dead organic material from the aquarium regularly—otherwise it will foul the water.

10 The use of medications to treat fish diseases also stresses the plants. After the treatment, carry out two partial water changes two days apart, changing one third of the water each time, and temporarily add fresh activated carbon to filter the rest.

HOW-TO: PLANT CARE

Caring for Tiger Lotus

Nymphaea lotus is a beautiful plant in the aquarium as long as it forms some attractive submerged leaves. Unfortunately, Tiger Lotus tends instead to produce only floating leaves that drift on the water surface and cast a considerable amount of shade in the aquarium. However, Tiger Lotus can actually be trained to produce more submerged leaves: To do this, routinely pinch off floating leaves—recognizable by their elongated leaf stalks—right at their base as they develop. In time, the plant will form very decorative, broad, submerged leaves on short leaf stalks, which are a real eye-catcher in the aquarium.

Cutting Back a Stand of Plants

Stem plants must be pruned from time to time, otherwise they develop unsightly leafless stalks. They will tolerate even radical pruning as long as at least two pairs of leaves are left on the part of the plant remaining in the substrate. Shorten the individual plants with a sharp pair of scissors. Be careful, though, that you don't simply cut back all the plants in a group to the same height. That looks very unnatural. It is better to prune back the plants on the edges somewhat more than those in the center.

Plant paths: Pruning is often used in maintaining plant paths. These are defined as a group of plants of the same species that completely cover an elongated, usually narrow area. Plant paths are a wonderful way to give structure to an aquarium. They draw the observer into the aquarium, or else simulate gently rising terrain by having the individual plants increase in height from the foreground of the aquarium towards the back.

Cuttings: The upper parts of stem plants which have been trimmed off are called top cuttings. You can use them to rejuvenate and propagate your plant community with ease (→ page 50).

Cleaning the Gravel with the Aquarium Vacuum

Pet stores carry various types of aquarium gravel vacuums. You can use them to rid the top layer of the

Individual stems are cut back with a sharp knife.

Aquarium gravel cleaners are very practical for removing mulm.

substrate (no more than 1 cm [1/2 inch] deep) of mulm, a mixture of uneaten food, feces, and other organic material which can seriously foul the water.

Separating the mulm from the gravel:
Take advantage of the regular weekly water change to clean the substrate at the same time. Attach the hose to the gravel vacuum. As you siphon off the water, mulm and gravel are stirred up. Since the gravel vacuum has a rather large cross-section, though, the flow velocity in it is low. The heavier gravel falls back to the bottom, while the mulm remains suspended and is siphoned out of the aquarium along with the water.

More Tips on Plant Care from the Experts
Cutting back large vallisnerias:
Even in the aquarium, leaves of vallisneria (→ page 18) can get to be over a meter (3 feet) long and then continue to grow, trailing across the water surface. This is very decorative, but often casts too much shade. Here it helps to trim back the individual leaves. But never prune off more than one third of the leaves, or you'll weaken the plant too much.

How to root adventitious plantlets:
The adventitious plantlets of Radicans Swordplant (*Echinodorus cordifolius*, page 15), which are similar to the slips at the ends of runners, should not be detached from the flowering stem too soon—otherwise they will have difficulty taking root. It is better to press them into the substrate along with the flower stalk, thus maintaining the connection to the "mother plant." Only after the young plants have developed roots and at least four leaves should the flower stalk be clipped off and removed—then the daughter plants will continue to grow quickly on their own.

Pinching off the floating leaves encourages **Tiger Lotus** *to put out submerged leaves.*

I N D E X

New leaves of Echinodorus osiris are reddish brown in color.

Associations:

Aquatic Gardeners Association (www.aquatic-gardeners.org)

Book for Further Reference:

James, Barry. 1986. *Aquarium Plants (A Fishkeeper's Guide).* Blacksburg, VA: Tetra.

Rataj, Karel, and Thomas J. Horeman. 1977. *Aquarium Plants: Their Identification, Cultivation and Ecology.*

Scheurmann, Ines. 1993. *Aquarium Plants Manual.* New York: Barron's Educational Series, Inc.

Stadelmann, Peter. 2000. *Setting Up an Aquarium.* New York: Barron's Educational Series, Inc.

Stodola, Jiri. 1967. *Encyclopedia of Water Plants.* Neptune, NJ: T.F.H. Publications, Inc.

Magazines for Further Reference:

The Aquatic Gardener Journal of the Aquatic Gardeners Association, c/o Jack O'Leary, 71 Ring Road, Plymptom, MA 02367-1406

Tropical Fish Hobbyist, T.F.H. Publications, Inc., Neptune City, NJ

Aquarium Fish Magazine, Boulder, CO

Web Sites:

www.aqualink.com
www.aquaplant.org (lots of links and searchable plant database)
www.aquatic-gardeners.org (web site of Aquatic Gardeners Association)
www.thekrib.com (aquarium site with lots of links)

About the Author

Wolfgang Gula grew up with aquarium science. After an apprenticeship in horticulture, he took over his father's aquarium plant nursery in 1986. In addition to selling aquarium plants and equipment, he was involved in developing new techniques for improved simulation of natural conditions in the aquarium. Since 1996 he has also been active in conducting training seminars for the pet trade.

The Illustrator

Johann Brandstetter was trained as an art restorer and painter. As a result of research expeditions with biologists in Central Africa and Asia, he switched to illustrating plants and animals. For many years he has been doing illustrations for well-known natural history publishers in Germany.

Photo Credits:

AQUA PRESS/Piednoir: pages 6/7, 9, 16 bottom right, 17 top left, bottom left, 28, 64/inside back cover; Bork: front cover large photo (fish), small photo; Kahl: front cover large photo (plants), pages 4/5, 8, 13, 16 top left, 17 bottom right, 20 top right, bottom left, bottom right, 21 top left, top right, bottom left, bottom right, 24, 33, 37, 45, 49, 52, 57 large photo, 61; Kasselmann: pages 17 center left, 20 top left, 21 bottom center, 48, 53; Nieuwenhuizen: page 2/3, 16 bottom left, 29, 41, 56; Peither: inside front cover/page 1, pages 12, 16 top right, 17 top right, 25, 32, 36, 40, 44, 57 small photo, back cover.

English language edition © Copyright 2002 by Barron's Educational Series, Inc.

© Copyright 2000 by Grafe und Unzer GmbH, Munich, Germany

Original German title is *Pflanzen furs Aquarium*.

Translated from the German by Mary Lynch.

All inquiries should be addressed to:
Barron's Educational Series, Inc.
250 Wireless Boulevard
Hauppauge, NY 11788
http://www.barronseduc.com

International Standard Book No. 0-7641-1926-5

Library of Congress Catalog Card No. 2001092832

Printed in China
9 8 7 6 5

EXPERT ADVICE

Experts answer the 10 most common questions about your aquarium plants.

1 How large should an aquarium be?

2 How should a newly installed aquarium be planted?

3 How deep can an aquarium be if it is equipped with fluorescent tubes?

4 How deep should the substrate be?

5 Is it enough to feed aquarium plants exclusively with liquid fertilizer?

6 How long should the aquarium lights be left on every day?

7 What about the aquarium gravel?

8 When is carbon dioxide fertilization a good idea?

9 Can I heat my aquarium using only an undergravel heater?

10 Can the lights be turned off for a few hours during the day and then be left on longer in the evening?